Published in Great Britain in 2015 by Wayland
First published in 2010

Text copyright © Pat Thomas 2010
Illustrations copyright © Lesley Harker 2010

Dewey number: 158-dc22
ISBN: 978 0 7502 9428 7

10 9 8 7 6 5 4 3 2

Wayland, an imprint of Hachette Children's Group
Part of Hodder & Stoughton
Carmelite House, 50 Victoria Embankment
London EC4Y 0DZ

Wayland Australia
Level 17/207 Kent Street
Sydney, NSW 2000

Concept design: Kate Buxton
Title design: D-R-ink

Printed in China

An Hachette UK Company

www.hachette.co.uk

www.hachettechildrens.co.uk

I Can Make a Difference

A FIRST LOOK AT SETTING A GOOD EXAMPLE

PAT THOMAS
ILLUSTRATED BY LESLEY HARKER

WAYLAND

Every person in the world is a teacher.
Even you. Did you know that?

Every day we teach each other how to do things. And we learn from each other too – even if we don't always know it.

7

When we watch someone, and copy the things they do,
we are learning from their example.

If we copy people who set a good example,
by behaving well and treating others with kindness,
that is how we will learn to behave.

And if we copy people who
behave badly, and treat others unkindly,
that is how we will learn to behave, too.

The best way to set a good example is to treat others
the way you want them to treat you...

...and to take care of your family, your friends and your home in the way you would like others to take care of them.

Some people set good examples
for us all in the work that
they do.

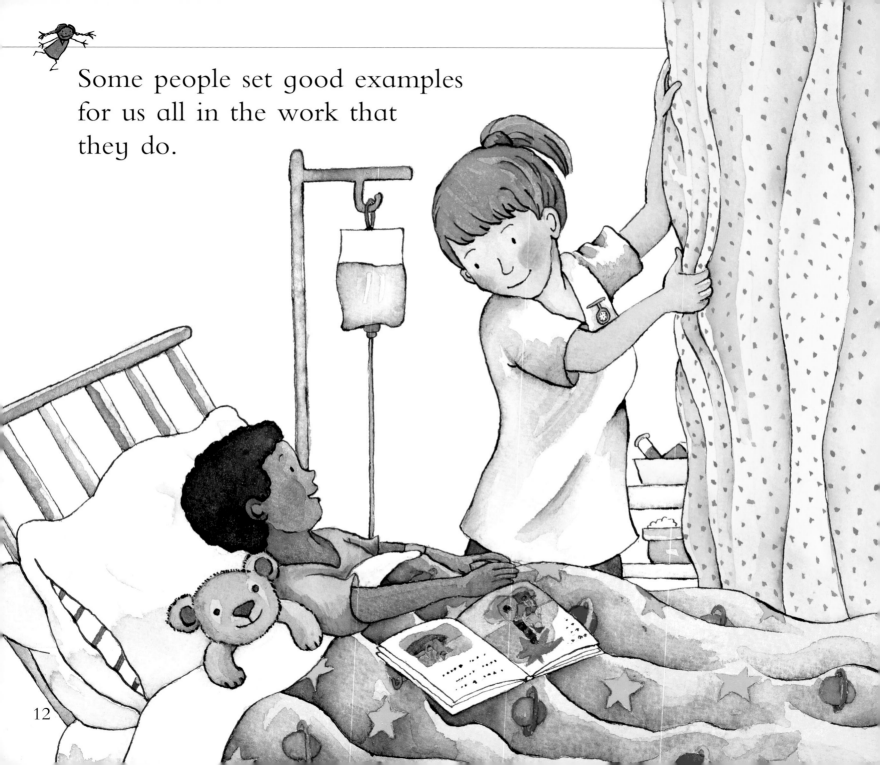

But all of us can find ways to set
a good example every day.

13

You can set a good example by saying 'please' and 'thank you', never calling names and offering to help...

... or by protecting those who are smaller or weaker than you, and helping to keep things clean and tidy.

You can help by carrying the heavy things,
not throwing rubbish on the ground, congratulating
the winning team, or reading to a sick friend.

What about you?

Can you think of some people who do jobs that set a good
example for us all? Can you think of some ways that you
might set a good example?

It's not just about taking care
of others, though.

You can also set
a good example by
taking good care of yourself.

Nobody's perfect all the time.

We all make mistakes and
every once in a while we all do
things and say things that aren't very nice.

When that happens saying
'I'm sorry' – and meaning it –
is another way to set
a good example.

19

Sometimes you might wonder why
it is important to set a good example.
Especially when you see other
people who never do.

20

You might also wonder if the way one person acts can really make a difference. Lots of adults wonder this too.

What about you?

Can you think of some times when you have seen other people setting a poor example? What happened? How did that make you feel?

Every person on earth has a choice about how they behave and how they treat others.

By setting a good example, and doing your best, you are teaching other people to act the same way.

And if those people copy you, then everyone they know will also learn this important lesson.

When everyone tries their best to behave well, it makes our families, our classrooms and our communities nicer places to be.

It makes working and playing together easier
and more enjoyable.

Most people who choose to be kind and polite to others want to make the world a better place.

It's like planting seeds in a garden.
The more you plant, the more beautiful
the garden will become.

27